WITHDRAWN

S
T
R
A
I
G
H
T

STRAIGHT

Poems 1971-1975

by
Richard Friedman

THE YELLOW PRESS — CHICAGO — 1975

Acknowledgements: Some of these poems have appeared in *Jukebox Poems*, Oink, Chicago, Out There, Boink, Buffalo Stamps, The Chicago Review, and The Milk Quarterly. Thanks to their editors. Many thanks also to Gail Angell, Ted Berrigan, Carol Lipsey, Peter Kostakis, Rochelle Kraut, Alice Notley, Mahadeva, Don Nisonoff, Neil Hackman, The Body Politic, Paul Carroll, Bob Holman, Darlene Pearlstein, Maxine Chernoff, Bob Rosenthal, The United States Postal Service, Mike Messer, Paul Hoover, Tom Joyce, and my parents.

Library of Congress Catalog Card Number 75-34702

ISBN 0-916328-00-7

The Yellow Press
2394 Blue Island
Chicago, IL 60608

Back cover photo by Alan Bass.
Cover conception by the author / Design by George Mattingly

for Darlene

CONTENTS

FROM THE VORTEX

I lift my voice aloud
make Mantra of American language now,
pronounce the words beginning my own millenium,
I here declare the end of the War!

— Allen Ginsberg, *Wichita Vortex Sutra*

I.

I too once declared the war over.

But I let my radio convince me
that my proclamation was unheard.
Then it was "Sporadic fighting brought
the total of American dead for the week to 330."

"Angelic Dylan" was absent.
James Brown entreated me to
"Say it loud, I'm black and I'm proud."

Calls to the station went unanswered.

I had no choice but to unplug the radio,
throw my watch out the door, raise the shade
and enter the vortex.

As Sherlock Holmes placed a bust in his window
to attract bullets and poison darts,
I left a surrogate in my bed.

II.

I vowed to meditate on the word "muni"
for silence is untranslatable
and Paul Muni could never be imitated.

I read only the last pages of books
to see how I might finish my own.

My mother was not destroyed
by the Kansas heart of America.
She was Hecate, the sorceress,
who relayed my thoughts to the gods
and prepared me for my journey
by discussing Kafka.

As she left, the Eagle,
tired of "beating his wings over Asia,"
came into the room to talk
in the language of feathers.
        I felt secure in his presence,
        but wary of his power.
Would he tear at my navel to taste my lint
or offer a flight mechanism for gentle stroking?

        Weeks after this meeting
        I expelled him from my body
        with convulsions,
        determined to enter Asia in peace.

III.

I shared my heartbeat with
the juice of freshly cut roses.
My thumb and forefinger met at the slanted ends
to produce four new buds
in simulation of my hand.

        In the vortex such events are common.
        Sharing takes place as in the stream
        shared by Mexican women washing
        first their clothes and then their bodies.

I washed under the blue-green
waterjet of a showerhead.
A mosquito on the plastic curtain
threatened to draw my blood,
but I would not draw his.
I could picture shattering a limb
and watching the injured body fly away.

A trapped animal will always
strive for release from restraint.
If necessary he will sacrifice a leg
by gnawing it off with his teeth
to escape the trapper's axe.

IV.

So now they say we're de-escalating
                    slowing down
                          winding down

        the war.

        I exit the swirling Ocean Vortex.

Here I live surrounded by the snails and algae
of my aquarium life.
No longer do guppies dart through my fingers;
diatoms and plankton have been sucked up
by the now herbivore barracuda.

I now communicate slowly and deliberately,
selecting meticulously
from among the twenty-six characters
who inhabit the universe of my language.

Winter 1971-72

MAHADEV

Giving "Earthspan" its first good listen,
on the occasion of the season's first snow:

On the rolling white sea
                snowy wave after wave
collides with the Earth,
as if surprised they were not allowed
                      to fall forever.
I could fall forever
              through the music
and be amazed to find
a soft bed of white sand
              to absorb my fall,
gently reminding me,
              "it's time to lay down your book
and see the words painted by the waves."

Yes, in October
             green turns to white,
catching city trees
in various states of undress,
             Big Sky laughing,
singing, "that's why I take the high road,
                  brother!"
Brother Mark,
            mirror image of myself,
why have you chosen the high road?
Remember celebrating
           events such as these
together, dancing to the fiddle,
focusing on the spaces between the snowflakes,
believing the jade and obsidian
              sunfalls of winter
were real? Perhaps you know
what's real now,
         a distinction we had trouble making,
or made trouble having
           on successive days.

Good luck, friend.
    May you live in the open air
as I inhabit open streams
wondering if you know better than I
why the snow has stopped
     and brothers drift apart.

October 18, 1972

INKSPOTS

living in the second week
    of a hay infusion
we are inkspots
            minor nodules on the gland of history
we are burrs
        but we do not prick
        and do not spurt
          (for you)
here we live with our many
    new friends and acquaintances

an independent free state

            a New Colony!

we are just down-home folks
letting our suspenders down
to visit your tactile responses

    wherever you touch
    we look back at you   the blank
                  stare of
                    holes

the incantations of an evening
with your precinct captain
swell and we sweat
through your clothes

    every itch has its spot

   the focal point of irritation
   from which the inflamed area radiates
        like dump trucks bouncing down
                bumpy roads

we are the anarchy of reading
    the experience of politics
       in a rural area

Yes
        the abyss *is* everywhere
and we inhabit it
        with our A-frame bodies
          and empty hearts

with Bob Rosenthal

SEDUCTION

It is said
that if a man
is able to keep
a woman awake
until three in
the morning — she
will be his.

So it is
with me &
my muse.

If I can only
last until three
without retreating
to sleep &
donating my words
to the restless
void of my dreams,

I will wake
the next day
with my note-
book open to an
ink filled page —

a poem to live
as testament
to my endurance.

CHRISTMAS POEM

for Darlene

Here again,
               as you sleep

        beneath the undersea world

                of the emerald (city)
            comforter / bedspread

                     in the bedroom.
I'm watching "The Fox"
         save the lives of some innocent people
                on television,

        if anyone can be innocent on television —

            tho these are just actors,

        far removed from the families
                you would serve Christmas dinner,

            and the children
                  whose lists you would fill,
            if you could

and if the priorities
            and crises
       of your daily life
               didn't monopolize
         your energy.

I'm lucky you're here to help me

           write these word lists
              I call poems,

         sending your love my way

                today and every day

       as we live together
              in our bathysphere apartment
        on the second of three storeys,

                        descending with the news
        every night
                    and rising (I hope)
    a little higher

                upward each morning.

                                December 24, 1972

BIG TED

for Ted Berrigan

Darlene's magnificent four
foot high papier mache over
chicken wire Dubuffet
yellow blue red & black
all easy over white
domesticated Panda Bear
is no less noticeable
than you — but after
a while you both
become part of the fur-
niture. You in your
pale green overflowing arm
chair at Ed Dorn's old
Diversey Mansion; Anselm
George Berrigan an infant
adornment, most boisterous
product of your middle
years, faces the unsavory
prospect of losing Mother
Alice's flowing breasts
forever — electric current
of maternal white
lightning leaving his mouth
to become rooted within

his now forming cranial
computer bank. Milk
deposits withdrawn by
baby now from bottle
only, someday from a
glass like school children,
perhaps with coffee like
school teachers too.
Milk Quarterly and its
children are also in
a way offspring of the
same parents. Meher Baba
tells us that when
we are in need of
a specific teacher,
not to worry about
catching jet plane to
see him, but to wait
and he will come
to us when we are
ready. So you came
to Chicago when we
needed you, heard
our lessons, recited
your own and left
the rest to us.
Now you repose
with splendor, a

not archaic Bell
Bottomed Buddha, en-
joying the Windy
City's ever rising world's
tallest buildings,
waiting for the
phone to ring.

January 8, 1973

DARLENE'S BIRTHDAY

The deep red rose

in your birthday bouquet

unfolded today,

signaling sister carnations,

pom poms & daisies:

"it's time to make things more fragrant in here!"

Outside, the January heat

record's breaking —

a new TOP TEN SMASH

for your 21st.

The escalator at the el

functions for the

first time in months

as I go to school / or

now that I'm teaching,

to work.

MY PROCLAMATION:

NO CLASS TODAY — MAGNIFICENCE!

The bare bones

of new buildings

going up   let the breeze

thru

as the cranes   bob &weave

obligingly,

& Muhammad Ali

ain't got nothin' on me

today.

Even the Aragon

contains
   fresh air,   preparing

         for an invasion of body snatchers
             tonight.

They won't seize me
        or you,
     tho we took each other's soul

   there three years ago.

           A tiny yellow butterfly

      opens its spotted wings,

    flying out of our bookcase,

      time for its
      season in heaven —

We'll not need Daniel Webster
   to retrieve it from Satan,

     it's ours to donate
        wherever.

Tomorrow they sign
  THE PEACE PACT,
      but we can't be complacent —

    there's this funny little hedgehog
     always whispering in my ear

    keeping me in line.

Yesterday you invoked
  "My Boyfriend's Back":

    "If I were you
    I'd take a permanent vacation!"
Well,
   you are

     SO LET'S GO!

And forever we'll fly
    together we'll glide
joyously taking
     another free ride.

MORNING AGAIN

One month from my
22nd birthday — this
must be my day.
In a rush, the
ocean of horrible
black cloud cover is
pulled back like
the sheet Darlene is
about to leave behind
revealing angelic white
alto-cirrus clouds and
wonderful faintly opaque
raspberry blue sky.
No more deadly nightshade!
Welcome in beautiful Lady
Day accompanied by
Phoebus' red fire engine.
The morning's first bird
lit on the lamp post
and extinguished
the light. If I spend
too much time on this
I'll let go before all
those nigger clouds leave town.

Progressively larger camels
caravan thru the Eastern sky.
An old woman exits
from the left doorway,
7728, at the same
time a young man
of 18 exits from the
right doorway, 7722.
They walk slowly towards
the center of the court-
yard, she dressed in a
dark grey wool overcoat,
he in a bright orange
jumpsuit. They meet in
the middle, she gives
him the key to the City,
does an about-face and
returns to her doorway.
He takes the key, turns
90° to his right, heads
down the sidewalk
and goes to work.

NO! The bad guys (black
clouds) move back in, I
can't control it — you
can't have your day & write

about it too. I'll just
fade back into the side-
lines — this must be
somebody else's day.

February 21, 1973

PROCESSIONAL

The gasping winter's last big snow
conspires to cement that yellow Chevy
                              in its parking place.
A cruel shock
                   for early buds
& over-anxious worms.

Brother Radiator —
                         you are far too wise
to head North after last week's warm spell,
& Landlord Bill is again a step ahead
                              of the elements,
tho the walkway around the courtyard
will provoke a sore back.
When we were looking for an apartment
he didn't ask if we were married,
but boasted instead of his roach control methods.

This June, three years later
                    & an entranceway West,
we are getting married,
                         but outdoors,
free from ceilings & walls.

Beneath the snow,
                    after 17 years of slumber,
millions of locusts, "cicadas,"
are stretching new legs & readying
                              their onslaught.
Since I was five, I've sworn
                         to be in another country
when they came back — when our handyman
cut the grass in '56
vacant shells & groggy insects
                         were churned to pulp.
Perhaps pollution has destroyed
                    the larvae, a lost generation
caused by increased radiation in the earth.

No matter, at 22 I tell myself
I've outlived running from my fears
& have learned the art of simple adaptation.

Let the Song of the Cicada
join that of our friends & family
to orchestrate the celebration
                  & complement our marriage vows.

March 17, 1973

POEM

Head a mile

        over page

   recurring dream: thumb is a walk away

                           from eyes

        focus: proceed towards thumb

                       get lost
                 in whorlmaze

  an exploitable sensation: being fingerprinted

                             busted:

        turned in by freaked sophomore
           caught in bio class,
     for dispensing acid

   Tripping — so far away now

               all (actual) souvenirs gone

 mental impressions rubbed in, not

           easy to get out

     Waiting

   allergy shots: 1 in each arm

        left: housedust right: ragweed

perpetual cold part of my personality

           handkerchief out

  "Oh, you've still got that cold?" or

      "You've got another cold!"

   same difference

I hadn't even noticed —

why waste time

belaboring the obvious?

But isn't that our national pastime?

Well, baseball is just alright with me

the slow

the boring

yes,

but plenty time between pitches

for composing lines of verse

deploying brain troops

into action —

Bill says fast sports are better for contemplation,

they keep your eyes & body busier —

EACH TO THEIR OWN METABOLISM!

That's it!

Yep, this must be

my METABOLIST MANIFESTO —

I'll have to call it "POEM"

so I won't be the last

to know.

SUBMERGE & EMERGE

A winged car
              splashes thru
                        the raintrenched alley

What does he think this is

      THE MINDANAO DEEP?

Summer heat has
        put the slug on the city

           again, atmosphere heavy
                 up to 35,000 feet —

Good Chance
           to break / wake
                  out / up
          in a sweat
                w/o moving

Piercing air conditioners provide
                muzak — is this

      intended to be
            singing aum

      of the universe —
               a wall
            of impenetrable quirks?

Sunshower at five o'clock
        punctuated the day,

    moon apostrophes the night
            & I light up
        when she holds me tight

           City windows are up
      for flo-thru ventilation —
           I never knew breathing underwater

    was so easy /

23

FISH!

"Have you got any threes?"

"Sure,
there's Bob, Don & Peter

Graymalkin, Sunspot & Milk

here

does that give you a book?"

"Well, three,
I know you're holding out on me!"

"Forget it,
trees grow more at night . . . "

"They figure nobody's watching . . . "

"Well, they aren't,
take me for instance —

goodbye beard

hello chin

new shoes

getting married —

got myself a whole new act"

"Right, & good luck to you!"

ACTION SUSPENSION

Darlene sewing ten feet away
                    my heart a constant throb
          could be
                    in another dimension, tho inseparable
from this present,
                    from this apartment
          into cat's eyes
                              a steady purr
This is how I always want it
                    Bob on the phone
          "packed a lot of living into one day"

                              just back from Iowa
Gail's paintings
                    white, purple, reds & greys
          wish I had a message for her
                    that would change her life
                                   for eternal better

years now I've known
                    I couldn't re-do anyone instantly
          they won't let you
                              & shouldn't
          but my sisters
                    must know I love them from afar

I'm realizing now
                              "No, I can't stop typing!"
          things as they are now
                    must be catalogued

     Bob & Shelley out to New York soon

     parents on a slow fade
                              Don somehow unapproachable
               or me
This Kelly green carpet can't last long

          summer will end

                    & then out on the street
                                          no job
          Peter falling into trap
                    as I leave it

                air tonight perfect
                          floats entire room
                                     into my heart

My poems always occur
                    on the page
          that's the way
                    I work
tho the ingredients
          meet before going in

          it's really up to them
                    if they didn't put me in gear
                              I wouldn't be here

          Now Don's on the phone

               "there's a party on my bus tonight,
               I'd like you to be there"

     "Here, talk to Darlene,

               I can't talk now."

          She can't decide if he's serious or not
     now she's mad 'cos I wouldn't talk

                    "Even Don said you sounded
                              like a dragoff!"
You'd think she could tell
I was doing something important
                         I'm still suspicious
               she's not involved with my writing

          maybe 'cos she's detached from her own too

          Instructions to meet
          at the Berwyn el at
                         10:27, 11:37 or 12:37

Bob knew,
          friends came over to preclude

me saying
              "sorry, I'm trying to write"
as if having to say it
                    ruins the result
Expectations for product now

                         Total Love to Anger

                              & back again

                a necessary regeneration

Unidentified bug on page

          attracted no doubt by electric hum

There he is on the back
                  on my thumb
                        & to oblivion

          On open French window sill

                    two cats observe the process
              become part of it
                        don't even know, care

                  they're never alienated from
                              their environment

Worry:
          I can't write about anything except myself

    & personal works require

at least two minor revelations
                    & they don't come easy!

Another:
          my works are too clear,
                    obvious & lack obscurity

I guess it's really that
          they (my poems) are so straightforward
          on the surface
                    so as to be obscure
                    underneath

                         SO WHAT!

Now we're back-to-back

typing & sewing

alcove all sold out

Catalogue over

Rip out the proper page
& send in your order!

FOR BOB AND SHELLEY'S WEDDING

Sleep well tonight starlings!

Today is an Independence Day
Achieved by singing your declarations
Of mutual love and dependence

I hope all is clear above
And so shall remain
For Bob and Shelley always

Aware of each other
Awake to the possibilities

Of a life which must be
Met alone, but is

Lived together

July 5, 1973

SUMMER OF NO POEMS

for John Wieners

Finally awake here
in the summer
of no poems,

sun's about to
come up & I'm
ending a personal

drought of too
many weeks of sleep
& relaxation —

friends also caught
in this plague
of no words; just

cause the TV wears
a hat, am I
supposed to call

it brother? And
these newly arrived
gnats here to in-

spect the overhead
light, last outpost
of a stormy monday,

they can't do more
than say hello &
doze off in the

bowl of the glass
protector & join
their fallen comrades.

To acknowledge their
presence at all
seems a sign of

desperation for fit
material, sitting on
cat-battered couch

revealing original skin
(green), two cushions
over from the wedding

pictures — red star
shirt w/ bow tie
haunts me from closet,

walks living room floor
w/o me as I sleep,
suede cowboy boots

boxed in dropping sand
on the carpet when
I turn over, gold

ring at bedside
misses my finger,
wakes ten minutes

before me to slip
on as I reach
to shut off alarm.

An ambulance passed
on my way to el,
first letter ever

from my father, in
Buffalo hospital, sleeps
uneasily as my hospital

letters to myself
still wait for
delivery & reply.

Morning birds echo
another day of clouds —
why should sun

come up at all
if it turns into the
wrong apartment at

the top of the stairs?
Another attempt to reach
thru the bars — how

did I get your book
in prison? Easy, I
escaped for a day &

had it sewn inside
my right lung so
all I breathe is you

& in a sense all my
words are yours too.
I agree, to accept sealed

bids for anything would
be premature right now
& besides, no

poem is admissable
evidence in the courts.
Signed / 6:00 A.M. 7-24-73

TOMBSTONE PIZZA CORP.

To test myself, I thought
about death for five minutes
today, and realized I
wasn't ready for it.

HYPOTHETICAL CONSTRUCT

for Bob Rosenthal

It's 2:37 somewhere
between Stevens Point &
you, as I'm sure
it is every night, but

this particular night
it's me who's filling
the gap by recognizing
& noting the fact.

You'll pick Darlene & me
up in about five hours
which places you in
the category of dreamer

most likely; as I can't
walk onto that stage,
throw off your lover
& impress upon you

that I want you to
have a happy birthday,
I'm communicating this
way — if the driver

dims his lights, the
sequence calls for brights
next, right now (car
past), later tonight or

sometime; after you leaving
for New York, the next
possibility can only be
us meeting again, there,

in Chicago, or elsewhere:
let's take that as given.
Let's assume also that
we'll not reach complete

understanding of each other
this weekend — then that
possibility for the future
is still open, right?

The most significance
I've found for your
23rd birthday is the
23 pairs of chromosomes

that help determine our
heredity, but I still
give us credit for
being able to pick

them off in our sleep.
In mitosis there is a
midpoint of alignment
after which two identical

sets of chromosomes are
formed from one — so if
that instant of communion
does occur, I look

forward, not only to seeing
you this morning, but
to being you
some other morning.

August 16, 1973

NAMAKAGON DAYBOOK

Decision made — when sleep would be easy —
To stay up and get it down —
      On porch, screens letting lake breeze
  thru — keeping bugs & twig-breaking animals out —
    at this point only a human would terrify.

Another day of reading Whitman aloud,
swimming clothesless, rowing about,
& loving each other, over.

Wind roars louder than any highway,
pulling it into my ears brings it on
stronger, semi-circular canals too, inundated
until all sense of balance is in the trees.

Things we saw today:

    Giant spider size of a salt shaker with
white cotton sack underside
    Sunset over the lake thru clouds — red
thru white & reflections on water
    A chipmunk hiding behind the freezer
at the general store
    A pinball get stuck between 10 points & a
bumper score & still no free game
    Each other naked
    The pier out of the water — thanks
to us — 500 lbs. of wet wood
    The hollow homes of bridge swallows — like
acoustical panels in a concert hall
    Tourists trolling for walleyes — no luck
    Moonrise thru clouds over the lake
    The Decline & Sinking of our air mattress —
slow leak
    Hummingbirds at Elmer's sugar red feeders

Things we heard today:

    Shelley screaming at Bob & vice-versa
    Tapes of Bob & me reading our new poems —
a summer's work in two weeks
    The wind everywhere
    Bob Dylan's "Copper Kettle," Hank Thompson's
"Humpty Dumpty"
    Darlene's yells for help — attacked by
a giant leech
    A wood duck quacking "thanks for the bread"
    The waves from a motorboat's wake hitting
us ear high
    And the motors

Things we did today:

    Ate lasagna
    Bought milk, pretzels, Mountain Dew, DeCon
    Made love
    Wrote poems
    Flushed the toilet (rarely) & jiggled
the handle
    Returned the rowboat to Elmer
    Sealed the pier for next summer
    Talked about where we stand vs.
the world
    Laughed a lot
    Got scared
    Went to sleep

NAMAKAGON OPERA HOUSE

Up here in Wisconsin:
Standing Room Only
For birches, maples & northern pines
An opera house with green
Tapestries up the walls and
Across the domed roof
Woodpeckers are hammering away
At new seats for the patrons
Phantom crickets play throughout
The performances given by
Mallards & swallows & whippoorwills
With the occasional
Falsetto of the hummingbird

After each act you can
Hear the applause rise
And fall with the wind
Through the trees

ON/OFF

On either side
of the music resides
a different disc jockey,
one now in limbo,
the other "on the air."
Turn over the record,
is the phone "on the hook?"
Lamps off, under covers,
hot female body, cold air
on top, warm underneath.
I've always needed a cool pillow
& a soft one at that.
Nightmares result from sleeping
on your arm. The Minotaur
can't dream well because of his horns.
I've given up hanging my clothes
up at night, socks fall
where they may, as do the pages
of the last night's book.
Alley door banging down (& out) there —
is some terrible derelict
about to become rich by completing
a hit on me for his tenth victim?
Locked doors won't stop a slug
from making an incision
in the bedroom window.
I'm sure the first
will shatter the Mexican's watercolor
at the black center of the cocoon
diffusing into yellow leaf.
Inside the chrysalis all is quiet,
a gentle dullness
similar to the snow-deadened alley.
But itinerant walkers could band together,
invade the interior lining of the bed
ripping inhabitants from sleep
prematurely like half-formed larvae.

"Alright, what is it now?"
Take what you want,
but leave the rest
for my weary body sleeping
in that bed across the street."

High on a mountain

of #2 bags

radio jazz
(hot)

above & thru

every empty slot

presorted & ready for delivery

*

Love vibration
of the mail

coursing thru the night

Somewhere there's a letter

IN TRANSIT

for everyone

*

The whole universe before you

*

Behind mirror slits:

"The Postal Inspectors"

on break too?

Why not put robots
w/ videotape eyes
back there

I wouldn't believe in them either

*

50 Stations — 50 Carriers

The one to one correspondence

of lunar rovers
to command modules

They'll always return

to THE MOTHER SHIP

as I do to work

& the edge of this envelope

returns to space

WINDOW SHOPPIN'

Window shoppin' from inside the window:

>> the hop & retract
>> of a squirrel on courtyard grass

Symmetry of 1920's three storey walkup

> Pre-winter lake light blue sky
>>>> Heavenly Blackboard

> for chalk white cloud
>>>> Instructions:

When walking outside avoid tunnels —
>>>> live on periphery
Cardinals are sacred,
>>> fly red arrows mating
Evergreens can teach
Dogs pretend, but cats own the streets
The crows will come for you if you fall
Sidewalks are dated,
>>> therefore temporary
When leaves sidle down
>>> like letters w/o their envelopes
> read 'em!
Sometimes home is in your feet
Don't forget the patrons who live in the trees
When sun's away
>>> let the comet light your way
Despite schemes & numbers,
>>>> humans don't move on rails
Winds are the best landscapers

ERASURE BY THE ELEMENTS
>>>> keep watching for further details

SICK LEAVE

He's got to give it to me

Disengagement from grinding cogs
of Postal Service Gear Machinery

"Deal me out today fellows,
you'll have to make it w/o me"

No doubt of that

The singular disappearance of each day's mail

swallowed by slots, boxes, secretaries & housewives

The terrible materialization of
tomorrow's paper w/o pity

Waiting for my grey pants w/ navy blue stripe
at 6:00 am

Government Usher

sworn to uphold the Constitution

& show each piece to its seat
in someone's house

Who knows what a letter sees:

the parts of a residence windowpaning
can't reveal

The pattern of family meals

Dressing to walk the dog
Master Bedroom in use
(nightstand perch)

On the best days
you see no one —

free to people each dome w/ ogres, nymphos,
murderers & teenagers as you will:

The face of Virgil Dice at 12:00

Sheriff Elrod cleaning his gun

The Police Superintendent mining
       his lawn

Goldberg, Goldenberg & Goldenberger
 trying to figure out who owns which kids
    on Sherwin St.

The inhabitants of Luna (ave)

Mike Royko driving his Datsun 280-Z down Sioux

Chester Lester leaving for work

Another day of life in Edgebrook District /

          zipped 60646

Cons inside the station now

        Sorting things out

kidding themselves they're doing it
  just for the money

I'd send 'em a postcard of my furlough /

      diurnal exile from their air space

  but I'll be seeing them all tomorrow

SPECIAL DELIVERY

Helping people realize my lifelong dream —
                              Mail on Sundays
       "No, I'm not a Venutian at your door,
       this is a special delivery letter for you!"

Most too stunned
                      to say thank you /
Newborn grandchild
           Death in the family?
                   no, the phone would announce that
           You owe $15,000 in back taxes?
                      More likely from the look on their faces

Just Remember, I'm just the messenger
                   Mercury in a beatup AMC jeep
In this case it's the song, not the singer

Parking jammed near Church
                              choir in full voice
It strikes me for the first time
that it might be fun to go to church
           or at least to have gone as a child

Closest I came was picking between
                              Jewish & Protestant
Services on Boy Scout weekend trips —
I felt obligated to choose — I just couldn't
                      sleep late in the tent

All those people inside the high ceilinged Basilica /

           Is some electricity more than copper
           conductor in middle of coins on the
           collection plate

                      passing from hand to hand?

       I'll never know

But they'll never know the power
       over human souls I carry —
                      Messenger of the Gods,
Winged Bearer of Momentous News.

MANUAL SURVIVAL

Behind gold armchair Sunspot nurses
Her litter of one
Under rocker sleeps Milk the father & milk
The result eight nipples
For one mouth
Should revert to my own neonatehood
Or become seven-headed
Catman of the Amazons:
Only male allowed to live
In the tribe
Forced to fuck all day
To prolong the race all male children
Are thrown in the river
Crocodile food after I've grown sterile
They'll choose a boychild to live
I'll have to care for him & raise him until
His first orgasm
Then he'll throw me
In the river that's why I've been learning
To sacrifice fingers to piranhas &
Regenerate appendages with the tincture
Of yellow ferns & serum
From the killer bees
I've persuaded a croc to bite my arm (left)
Off at the elbow cleanly
So I can paddle up river
(I must remember to cup my hand)
When his eyes open
The kitten can watch the accompanying
Gestures to my tale of escape
An epic of migration
Northward on the wings of silver
Butterflies moving too fast & invisible
For the netmouths of snow leopards
The poison purple darts of headhunters
Imagine the prize of seven
All dependent on one
Vulnerable heart

The copper breastplate staplegunned
Over my left nipple corrodes
From within the agent
Black orchid tattoo *Mother*
The fee of the open-heart surgeon
Makes this the world's most valuable
Human illustration
I know the conversion
Of certain common elements
Into nuclear reaction sources will soon
Obliterate most of South America &
Float this island apartment
Back into the realm of unclassified
Sense data but I still advocate
Population control
Even if it does cost three times
As much I say
Get Sunspot spayed
Let Milk retain his manhood

ADVICE

Disrespect
for those
you like
leads to
dismember-
ment of
your own
appendages.

CHANGE OF VENUE

New apartment
           new home
      same occupants inside:
                cats, Angell paintings
                Darlene & Richard
      The newlyweds
           one year later
    "The thrill is gone?"
            nope,
                just hibernating
        marking time

      "if you're just killing time,
      then you don't deserve to live"

Can life prosper
        in flapjack hirises?
      I'm three flights up
           & still them confounded

              cement icebergs
        tower above
"Look, my Gods are the sun,
        lake & sky"

      & if I'm walking a beat for bread
      that don't fill my brain w/ lead
  Alcove vista
      bamboo filter
    dictate &
      I record:

formula for torpedo sinking of the condominiums

elegy / ode for Hank Aaron's 715th homerun

strategy for interpreting Nixon's demise

        He knows Sleep

The Enforcer

Time locks

set
dream tumblers
body
click

jeweled room

cactus of tomorrow

SLICE OF

Disgruntled in the extreme /

                temporarily

      Home from work sick

                14 hours sleep

                        serrated

President Ford's press conference
      followed by
                biography/epitaph for Chas. Lindbergh

Need to commemorate events:

                Resignation of Nixon the Dreamkiller

                stripped of power to implode upon your
                sleep to politic for the belief "he's not
                such a bad guy" by discussing your family

      Previous Resignation of Agnew the Thick

      You can't plead "no lo contendre" to
      accusations of non-human ancestry

The Ascension of the Virgin / Gerald Ford

Almost subverting my obsessive need to
hate national leaders before appointing
Rockefeller the Power Buyer, Vice President

Day after Labor Day
                Darlene assumes teacher's position
        at South Side School — buildup
    of tension & fear will subside
                in a few weeks I trust —

      You just go in there
      & give the kids your best shot
                & hope it gets thru

Previous intentions of early retirement
                from P.O. seem frustrated

I mean it's hard to argue with
    "8 hours pay for five hours work"

After Midnight my time is not my own

    Prep for five o'clock upstart
    uniform on
    shoes ready to walk

    Mouth ready to squawk
        at mates

"The people on your route
    must feel lucky to get their mail
        in time for dinner"

    "I better take a sack out there
        to pick up all your misdeliveries
            from yesterday"

More hectic than lazy Wisconsin tempo

        chess with Bob

    frisbee in the lake
        non-stop eating &
    rejection slips for dozens
    of submissions to
        Milk Quarterly

Put these in the hamper
    (Flag Up) for the postman
  on his rural route
        He'll think we've friends nationwide

Battered red Datsun
    highways on rivers

        speed into thunderstorms
    rainbow at sunset

Organization inherent if destination obscured

Hope Darlene gets home soon

    there's plenty of parking

EPITHALAMION

for Maxine & Paul

They met at a poetry reading you know
"All Saint's Eve" for the Body Politic
The line is married to the page
As your car couples with a parking space

Every night you live between the lines
Of the poems written and lived that day
Maxine, I've been driving in the same car
With you for three years and we've

Never had an accident
That must be a good sign
Paul, you married me tuxedoed on the beach
It's only fair you read my words again

A poem for those of born divine
Joined in two hours on this sunlit Saturday
Blue October morning of decision
I've been married over a year & it's

Easier to say "Wife" than "girlfriend"
Or "roommate," the public
Will appreciate this simplification
Of their labeling process, but

That's their business and you're
Not here to make life easy for taxmen
Or even relatives who've been euphemizing
Your relationship for years anyway

But to say something to each other
That perversely still can't be communicated
Any other way — then again
I can't imagine any other way I'd have it

Getting to sip champagne and watch
Two friends kiss in the sky
Sealing a letter printed on air
Delivered on wind currents of love

THE BODY POLITIC

In the night kitchen

while Chicago slept

some nastiness cooked up

behind Oxford's Pub

Chili so hot they put the hoses to it

flames taste the flesh

of scenery crowds & costumes

After image of actors

Day of the Locust

floorboards warp & crackle

footlight parade of shades

dream sequences
replayed in the smoke

Audience burn & pine

For an encore The Fire Chief

provides dolphins w/ axehandles

shooting baskets on the stage

where Corso cussed & raved

"Alright you smart fuckers,
what was the first book?"

I'm not sure, but I'll bet
its pages curled to ash
when the Library at Alexandria
burned down

Oral Poetry & its Recitation

Immortal

Homer didn't have a typewriter

Words pass from ear to ear

lodging overnight in the head
between

Memory on all levels operative

Formerly the poetry reading was the only way
(no books)

If you didn't hear a poem you missed it

The politicos control publishing
(always have)

In person poetry the purest way

You & the poet one-on-one

HOWL — Allen Ginsberg — Fantasy 7013
Recorded Jan 1959
at Big Table Readings in Chicago

Now in Chicago it's here

THE BODY POLITIC — 2259 N. Lincoln

Readings on Monday nights

The only Series for our town

Steve Stone of the Cubs a poet

If you call yourself one you are

Too busy to argue the point,

but I've never seen him in the bleachers

upstairs where the floor creaks so bad
the act of leaving insults the poet

or in the workshop room where Wieners lectured
beautifully on Gay philosophy
& we danced after our Halloween Party / Open Reading
"All readers must be in costume!"

Most of the action downstairs
in the rug room / Alice Liddell Theater

where more than one

aficionado has siesta'd   during a slow set

"When I woke up I was two inches high"

That's the price you pay for snoring, Pancho

All power to the reader

    granted by you
                the audience

    without whom we wouldn't be here

        this whole place would be a Grand Canyon

gaping hole of performers
           talking to themselves

    it wouldn't be worth rebuilding

      like an abandoned Opera House
        in a ghosttown outside Phoenix, Arizona

or an art museum visited only by cameras

          what good would it be?

In fact, The Yellow Press should be paying you
          for attending these readings

    as should The Community Arts Foundation
          for attending their performances

    and we all are
          doing our best

to astound & enlighten you

        so humbly with hats in hand

    in this room of words
      unharmed by flames

we turn again to you for support

        asking only your money

    thanking you in advance

    The Body Politic

October 7, 1974

ANNIVERSARY DAY

One year later
             still a mailman
New President
             Nixon gone
   "I guess you all move up a notch now"

Seniority a myth

             Imagery a hoax

Life above all
   People to live it

             SPECIAL BULLETIN — "Nixon in critical condition"

First compassion for the man
I can't hold a grudge

                    Wish anyone's death
People close to me
                    near I know

No way to prepare
                    When you have to

Adapt you do

October 27, 1974

FOR RICHARD

Everybody wants to know
   If I've been writing

So what? If I did they wouldn't
   want to read it
       I wouldn't want to type it

& Lord knows I'm the only one

    who'd print it

But yes,
   I've been writing & it ain't on paper
& yes it's something different

& no I don't need to submit it
      to anyone

to know what it is

It's called:
    "The one clear point of concentration
    is dangerous, so be vague"

OFF DAY

    Guilt for sleeping past
The time I'd be done working
                    obscures the pleasure
Of the night before
             a day off
           from predawn arisal
I'm almost human again

I want to be irresponsible
                  undependable a follower
of uninterrupted sleep
           "Shut my phone off forever"
Give the overtime
        to the more deserving

Leave me my newspapers
        basketball & Earth Shoes
           because I walk
Out on you all
        Do it yourself
"Deliver it yourself, boss"

        Drive yourself there, man

I'm here alone
       with my wife & immediate family
Nobody else knows my name

The TV set cares more for me
        than you
I turn it on
        decide what channel it gets to watch
           which direction its antenna points

I'm up here in the tower
        w/ Joni Mitchell & Bob Dylan
Safe & Warm
       there's plenty of catfood
A liquid diet will sustain my life
          orange juice & Pepsi

It's Richard & Darlene
      setting feet
     for the sea of tranquility
Gravity down
    on the misunderstood
Sunlit side of the moon

WINTER WITHOUT SNOW

Alone in the
        emergency waiting room
Hospital my life
        just visiting not
Staying overnight
        the X-ray machines are
Waiting for the next Saturday
        night injury victim
I now the victim
        of forces uncontrollable
Attacking wife & father

Why don't they just
        give me a bed
And let me move in
        I'll park my car
Outside & rest my weary legs
        the absence of motion
Simple emotion
        of patient's pain
Can't classify what we
        on outside feel
Can't hard as I try

Intensify & absorb
        their pulse
Know their pain
        or ease its effect

CIVIL SERVANT

for Tom Joyce & Mike Messer

Car broke down again
Sitting in front of my building
While I'm out on the street
Freezing trying to hitch into work —
To think at 5:30 A.M.
The combination of my extended thumb
And the navy blue stripe
Down my grey post office pants
Does *not* produce a ride
Hey Volkswagen, you too secure
With one all purpose person inside —
Operator — passenger — cosmic rationale
For your appearance on this street —
No room for me?
And you, Cadillac, those bench seats
Could hold four across, one
Third of a jury or judge, defendant
And the opposing attorneys
Oh forget it / my 55¢ entitles
Me to my own seat
On this bus of my city
Even if it's just the driver, me
And forty-six transparencies going
Down Devon in the predawn air
Yeah, that's alright, this little
Piece of paper's my transfer
Good for this hour on
Any other of the Mayor's vehicles
This bus my second this morning
To the end of the line
And walk on in from there
Sure, I know my little Eisenhower
Jacket w/ the Post Office Eagle
Would've given the drivers
An excuse to pick me up "heh, heh
The mail must go thru," but
Must I resort to a uniform

For admittance to their breathing space?
Isn't just my legs, head,
Arms & opposible thumb identifying
Species enough? Just keep
Trotting Henry, another mile past
The Sheriffs & Doctors whose mail
You'll deliver this morning, right,
The same ones who wouldn't
Have you in their cars, lies
The well-lit harbor of your team's
Loading dock, already full as you walk
In the door late but accepted & liked
Just another foot soldier in The Civilian Army

APRIL SNOW

for my father

This alcove a snow tunnel
Lucky only black letters
Can hit me in the face
                    Visibility Zero
When this hits a poet
                    It's worse than Kelvin's
Absolute Zero
              the absence
Of motion & heat

These sheets of metallic fragments
Disguised as snow
                hurt & burn till they cover
And then there's peace
For the streets & cars underneath
                  no more friction
Between them it's all over

Relieved of society's functions
              courtesy & love
For humans these never end

What you've invested in the world
Has a way of insuring its preservation
An absorption into the universe
                not dependent on memory
An Earth renewal
                of matter & energy we can't control
Tho it is controlled

And even doctors & judges submit
To a spring blizzard attended by lightning & thunder

A city stops when thorofares sleep beneath the snow
But we're awake as we were when we walked
In this world with spark in our step
And ready as we'll ever be to talk

The words spell themselves
And love keeps us going

OFF THE MAP

Hey listen
                there's a brook talking
        running under this cottage
                        and as for "babbling"
it's making more sense
                        than me

Driving sixty miles
in night blackened Smokies
                hairpin turns still
friction of rubber
                        to pavement in my head
eyelid vistas
                        of double yellow lines

What scared me most
was those Army Corps of Engineers'
        Dams trying to hold back
all that water & the stupidity
        of "harnessing nature's power"
with horrible
                        outposts of concrete
                        from another solar system

After the fourth
                        "just around the bend"
        I'd had 'em
                        wondering what galaxy
North Carolina belonged to
        and which claimed Tennessee

Hills & mountains
                        w/ valleys
        in between all under
                the reign of the TVA

At one juncture
        the map said FY
        but showed a road cross
                The Tennessee River

a dollar later the 260 lb. ferryman
        let our Datsun & us off
                on the other side
Charon in the guise of a walking stove
        but which side is which?
                they both smell pretty
    "You gotta go South to find spring"
    & green is the color of the day
                but black is the night

& I'm glad to be tucked in
        the double bed here w/ Darlene
in this
        cabin, *Sex In The Woods*
can't be surpassed
                for sheer joy
like taking topless photos
        from a swinging bridge
    over the falls
                & sighting woodpeckers doing
        their thing to a tree
                "Lights out for all you bugs inside!"
& fucking
            on a flat rock
        over a gulch
            at The Rim Rock Recreation Area
Sorry for the abruptness
            but it's a new outdoor record

Sounds of the Frigidaire
                nothing inside
        but cold shelves
            Darlene writing in bed
Why is paper so important to writing?
        I could go down the road
            to The Joyce Kilmer Memorial Forest
    & yell
                "Fuck You Joyce,
            every tree wasted printing
                your poems is a travesty!"
A senseless war crime
            on the order
        of Americans dying supporting Thieu in Vietnam

Now he's gone
     & that country will soon
   revert back
           to its people
 & that paper and this too
       will probably be burned
   to re-enter the universe
   in another form /
             solid to gas
this writing another solid
         recycled from thought based
     on matter imprint from eye
See
   there's no clocks in this place
It's great
     to live by your wits
   & mark time by the heavens
  even if navigation
    by stars eludes you
You've everything you need
        here but a sextant

The mountains are up
        in the morning
to greet you
     there's sun
   and a new
  grant of wonders
       to match.

SMOKEY MOUNTAIN MORNING

Porch a window up above
a creek in the Great Smokies
Clouds that know your name
You could shake their hand
and they'd be gentle, bees
that check you out quietly
before putting a buzz on, sun
warm in an undertow sense
heat sneaking up slow
pace of the morning, birds
out of the blue and into
the green they call home
I've gladly called this cottage
home these last two days
on vacation an anachronism
I mean it's all just life
uninterrupted / intervals
not that well-defined, tho
location plays a part
in spelling out the phases:
"You're in the mountains
of North Carolina it's
spring, breezes blow thru
your world of lilacs
and crocusses in bloom, and
we all breathe together,
delighted by the sweet
fragrance as we inhale,
singing as one as we exhale."

MAMMOTH CAVE

Outside the door to this cottage
The copperheads line up
Waiting to say hello
In the morning but
Little do they know

That thunder & lightning
Got a friend, tornado,
And she's gonna snatch
Us up with her windy claw
And take us to her house

On the other side of
The sun for breakfast
And there'll be no poison
There and the guided tours
Are free and leave every second

COPPERHEAD

You were sure to be feared
When you put that Lincoln mask on

WILDERNESS TRAIL

It's great living in fear
Of a deadly snake tugging
Your pants leg or a grizzly
Hugging you to death
For when the adrenalin flows
So do the brain juices
And word cascades hit
Your pages like falling rocks
Not to mention it's
A useful lesson in mortality

BACK IN THE SADDLE AGAIN

Wet Sunday return
to work after two weeks
away from my station
an infusion of gray
red, white & blue
jeep sloshes thru
one man swears he'll
have me on the carpet
Monday for splashing him
"you cocksucker, like hell
it was an accident!"
but there isn't any carpeting
at the P.O. and I learned
today that my two week absence
parallels that of the superintendent
in midst of a "nervous breakdown" —
"I talked to him on the phone
and he's like a popsicle,
exposed nerve, ready to explode,
he sounded like a little kid"
and I felt like a kid
myself delivering a special
delivery package & a letter
to a young Polish woman
and discovering in the jeep
it was a five dollar bill
she had pressed into my hand

WALKING BY MYSELF

The halfmoon
                    said "Howdy"
          this morning as I went in
for a halfday of work
                        (thanks boss)
    Hardest was losing
                        flipping quarters / odd man wins
                    on the loading dock
No sleep
          now grant
        together   "Give me $7,500 please"
            It's In
                    Downtown, how I love
Downtown Chicago,
                        peculiar to me among my friends
Where else
            does sex ricochet
        off every gray cornerstone
do noisy elevated trains
                        circle the square
        The thrill
                    of using a perfect xerox
            meeting a former lover's sister
            & not asking about her sister
The joy
        of parking underground
        & visiting w/ Monet
                        at The Art Institute
    "Just notice the light & water
                    your first time thru"
Too Much!
            like just watching TV antennae
                out el train windows
or just looking
            at people's shoes
        walking thru the exhibit
                    walking cross the streets

love for a blind man
                              "walkin' by myself"
the perfected
                    swinging the umbrella walk
the walk of rain clouds
                         in & out
                    the downtown
                                   revolving door
In walked a pair of caramel brown
                    handstitched sandals into the next stall
          first time in memory
                              in Art Institute john,
Nothing special,
                    but it does allow
          a certain pause
                         for reflection, an opportunity
To retrace my steps

DOWNTOWN CHICAGO

Love for people in an abstract sense

Hits you
        in the eyes
   down here
          & yes,
It's the way their eyes
        inhabit their bodies
  too that you love
And makes you love
           their bodies
As well
       Walking to the Garland Street
  Flower Stand
         to buy your mother
Some flowers
       you end up giving to your wife

RESIGNATION DAY

The slamming down of a badge
     on a desk or table proclaiming
             "I QUIT!"

I can't be sheriff of this town no more
     I'm finished here
          I give up
     my employment my position my retirement fund
    my health benefits the free life insurance
the cost of living escalator clause

all abdicated, abandoned, renounced
           a subway ride downtown
     to re-sign on the dotted lines
of official forms
       "This was just my hobby"
I surrender, submit, & forsake
     this USPS rider's permit, operator's license, the silver
                              star

rip the eagles off my shirts
     fly away w/ letters in their beaks
     I relinquish their guardianship
       along w/ the shine on my black shoes
     the rasp in my voice
           the 6 am circles under my eyes
That's right
     I'm leaving
  Here's formal notice in writing
Assume passive acceptance to the authority
      unresisting acquiescence to the right
of the mail to be delivered even tho I'm not there

AGAINST SOLIPSISM

    I'm all for the divine dispensations
Let them rain on me
      I'm Re-Zion & re: sign
   of a diminishing economic growth pattern

I'm through
                    Call me UNEMPLOYED
                        no, self-employed
by the annulment of the government's
                    Oath of Office
                        Pledge Allegiance Now To Thyself
        Civilian
                    Seniority Shattered
                                    an age of restoration
            Give me back my after midnights
My dawn as a sedative
                        my moon as a lamp face

                                            I'm back
                    fishing for "letters in my head
                        now, not
                        in my hand"   (letter of resignation)

following the
                    steps along the San Clemente Beach
            of ex-Nixon
                            ex-Agnew
                    gimpily traversing the moors

                                    ex-Golda Meir
            ex-Khrushchev
                        ex-Willie Mays

        ex-Thieu and the war dead of Vietnam

    but my last day was a triumph, a pleasure
I threw the same case
                    I'd started on
                    got the mail out on time

        fed my co-workers
                            & shook the collective hand
                    of all assembled
                                to remain their fate

            mine to resign
                        but not w/o tears
                    for the friends left behind

                            & the identity obscured

Now I'm just a man
            w/o prefixes
   a worker w/o a paycheck
                        a bed contains my tired head
            resting uneasy
                        for the ride west

Wagonmaster of my Soul
                  guide the wheels round
         may hands
                  of compasses & clocks
      register applause

                        these legs have just started walking

               this *poet*'s ready to roll

               June 20, 1975